The Flautist and the Flute

Poems of Life and Love, Despair and Hope, Music and Devotion

Sagnik Chakraborty

BookLeaf Publishing

India | USA | UK

What belongs to You, is dedicated to You.

Acknowledgement

I acknowledge the contribution of all those who have understood love as devotion and devotion as love in the core of their heart and have expressed this understanding through vivid verse, lucid lyric and mesmerising melody.

Preface

This poetic collection is conceptualised as an ardent expression of human emotions interlaced with divinity in everyday life. It is a lyrical attempt to underscore how life and love are intertwined at every step, how love is incomplete without devotion and vice versa and how — whether we realise it or not — the lover's heart and the devotee's heart are ultimately identical.

As someone who finds all things true, good and beautiful to be an essential expression of Krishna's love, this somehow becomes a leitmotif in most of my poetic works, subtly or otherwise. However, I also believe that our moments of pain, untruth, weakness and despair are equally manifestations of divinity. Pain leads to courage; untruth points out the necessity of truth; hatred reveals the requirement of love. For Vāsudeva is the Lord of the Innermost! He resides in the human heart as well as the heart of the natural world.

Thus, the transition from despair to hope and from grief to equilibrium plays a prominent part in the poetic expressions found within these pages, with the interplay between the human and the natural world along with the subtle omnipresence of divinity playing a profound role.

By a stroke of serendipity this collection of lyrical verses was concluded in Mathura, although I had no prior plans to visit the birthplace of Krishna on the particular day I wrote the final poem. It just happened!

I welcome every reader, especially those who share the belief that the human heart is a *mandir* and love is worship, to partake in this lyrical journey of celebrating the pining and yearning of the human heart, along with love for and of Divinity — within and without, seen and unseen, tangible and intangible.

For that is Krishna: the All-Attractive, the Centre of the Universe and the Centre of Love.

The Reed Flute

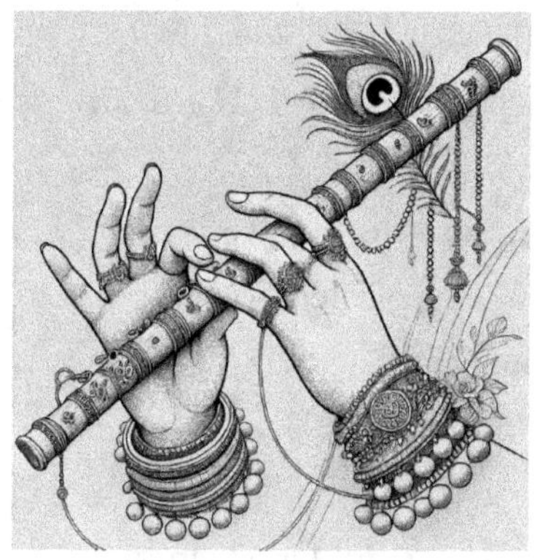

Once there was a bamboo reed,
Once there was a blade of grass,
There was once but a dormant seed,
There was once but a shard of glass.

An empty heart was all it had,
A pining soul its only good,
A blind man's goal was all it knew,
A futile start was all it could.

And then there came the breath divine,
Light, O Light! O lightning fierce!
A lilting voice that said, "You're mine!"
A smile that did embrace and pierce.

The smile! The smile that beamed so sweet,
Radiant on His lotus face,
His hands were lotus, lotus feet,
His glance poured forth His deathless grace.

Now there is a flute that plays,
Now there is a garden green,
A verdant tree that swings and sways,
A diamond with a sparkling sheen.

The reed flute shudders, trembles, weeps,
Ecstasy its whole heart sweeps,
The Master smiles, an enigma this,
The Flautist plays; the flute is His.

Night and Day

Darkness is the grave shroud of the Night,
And white light is the sceptre of the Day,
The Cosmic Soul gifts both a unique way
To sing their lore in hues pale and bright.
The golden sun ushers in the Day,
The moon and distant stars guard the Night,
Continuous is their cosmic flight,
Not Space, nor Time may lie still on the way.
Night and Day are entwined, conjoined twins,
One concludes, there the other begins.

Futility

With words I painted spring
So the cuckoo bird could sing,
Sing she did, but not in glee,
Her notes just yielded pity for me –
My crafted, worded toy
Failed to give me joy.

I pleaded Storm to hear,
This boat of mine to steer,
He took a portion, not the whole,
Of my rudderless, reckless soul –
In two my heart was torn,
In silence, grief was born.

The pearl from oyster shell
That's not to buy or sell,
In frenzied lust I snatched away
And wore as jewel night and day –
It caused my heart to fade,
And wither into shade.

I looked up at the sky
And cried to heavens high –
Return to me the virgin bliss
Of innocence green, which I now miss!
Not an answer came,
Futility is my name.

The Child

A little child I am, I know,
In innocence each day I grow,
The world I witness; curious eyes,
As each day dawns with a new sunrise.

I look, I listen, I love, I learn
What fame or money cannot earn,
For with each breath of my childhood
I teach Mankind what's pure and good.

Springtime Farewell

When soulfully the cuckoo starts to sing
Of rebirth, hope, and joy, and festive shower,
And nights of wintry chill fade from view;
While vernal clusters usher in the Spring,
It's then I hear my friend, a youthful flower,
Express a mournful, cruel, heavy, *Adieu.*

Before the season's prime dawn could shine
forth,
In grief wailed the nightingale of wild,
Before his impetuous petals bloomed,
A flower must bid farewell to home and
hearth,

The ancient garden of worldly life has sent
The missive of another vernal song,
(But) the blossom's youthful life is now spent,
A day too short? Was it an hour too long?

On a day when brightly smiled the sun,
I heard the silent whisper of my soul:
It's time; away from friends you must now
sail,
The Distant Friend, the Final Friend, He calls!

It is Spring

The flowers might be wilting,
It is Spring,
The mind might be fleeting,
It is Spring.
The pain might be seething,
It is Spring,
My heart might be bleeding,
It is Spring.

The one who moves so deep
my torrid heart
To ink these lines, so vivid,
(of me, a part);
May she be so distant –
a mere dream;
I see in me, still,
her visage gleam.

Speech might be dormant,
Love sleeps not,
Lyric shall now speak
And lend heart wings,
The song might be tethered,
It is Spring,
The smile might be withered,
Yet it is Spring.

Ditty of Desolation

When summer's fiery days end at last,
And vapoury clouds shroud the sky's visage,
The notes of *Malhar* quench a thirsty heart;
Alas, I hear the advent of a storm.

The winding river nurtures crops and dreams,
Her current brings joy unbridled to all,
Friend to lovers, Muse is she to poets;
I see in her a reservoir of tears.

The solitary traveller walks as evening falls
And delights in the glow-worm in the dark,
A tender-glowing gem in Nature's lap;
I fear the simmering fire in her heart.

The vernal riot of colours does express
Love and friendly affection for all,
A time it is for loving hearts to sing;
A time it is for broken hearts to sigh.

Urban Sunrise

The clouds play *Holi* in the scarlet sky,
I watch in wonder as a fresh day dawns,
The gushing blood in me a new life spawns,
A sweet-scented breeze goes wafting by.
I drink in with my eyes the sun's first rays,
A mellow melodic missive the heart can feel:
Nature's loving hands can all wounds heal
Through soft caresses of her divine breath.
(As) the sky welcomes the growing scarlet
tide,
And the night of darkness seeks to hide,
The forest greets the youthful morning
breeze,
The awakened flowers sporting with the bees,
The chirping birds fluttering with joy;
And humankind welcomes Life's envoy.

Summer and Monsoon

Grief is the Summer sun raining fire,
A fiery scourge that scorches body and mind;
In silence bides her time, beyond the pyre,
A joyous rebirth, under Monsoon's wind.
If pain is wrought in Summer's haughty heart,
It carries Monsoon's promise in a part.

Light in Darkness

In the wilderness,
drifting through the heart of darkness,
sifting through the layers of night,
The celestial crescent recalls
what seems to be a previous birth;

Reminded am I
of a brighter yesterday,
that shone with the light
of a thousand suns:
Your visage bright!

The fateful cycle
that mortals know as Time,
Carrying endless lifetimes,
remorseless births and deaths,
back and forth,

Yet pregnant with a promise;
Fierce, and pure, and true,
to behold and to feel,
in the core of my human heart.

Musings of a Young Guitarist

As I hold the chords and strum the strings,
    my guitar sings;

Passionate, I clasp it to my breast,
    its haven of rest;

My fingers kiss the notes that softly sound
    with joy unbound;

As they dance upon the tune they feed,
    my fingers bleed;

Yet sweeter is the music with the pain;
    the mild refrain;

And with it now, in harmony complete,
shall my heart beat.

The Birth of Love

Bright, temperate, and tender was the dawn,
And gentle was the rustling of the breeze,
When in the womb of Beauty Love was born;

Then, softly sounded murmurs in the trees,
Truth, in his bright-winged cape and
fluttering flight,
Rose to the heavens, in impetuous ease,

In eager zeal, the harbinger of light,
Did declare loud the advent of the New,
The precious gift of holy tryst of night,

When Beauty with Truth convened on green
dew,
And conceived was the fairest of the fair,
And truest of the true that all worlds knew.

For Love is born, and Love shall permeate air,
Water, land and space, and hearts that care.

The Strings of Heart

In my thoughts I forged a lyre
And softly fed it of my mind,
And tried to play many an air,
But lifeless was its kind.

With loving hands was strung the lyre
Yet, no sonorous note would ring;
Now that the lyre broken lies,
The strings of heart shall sing.

Vision of the Beloved

I fell asleep within my dream,
Cradled by the lonesome night,
Beyond the pale of time and distance
Shone your face, a vision bright!
I drank Love's hemlock in my dream,
And died upon your loving sighs,
(To be) reborn at the hour of daybreak,
As night closed her thousand eyes.

In the fierceness of dawn's beauty
Yet again I see you, Love!
Bright and warm as the infant Sun,
And serene as the sky above!

The eastern lights bring to the world
The gift of life, with bliss to part,
In dawn is sketched my Beloved's smile,
In light is etched her loving heart.

The Blue Hills Call

When the blue hills call and the sun shines
bright,
And the valleys green bathe in vivid light,
Expect me not, *O Moment*, to stay and tarry;
I shall but take off on a joyous flight.

With lungs filled full with fragrant air,
Downhill shall I race, with not a care.
Hold me not, *O Moment*, with words that
parry;
On wings of heart the winds I shall dare.

Away farther, into those blue hills
To meet again childhood as heart wills,
Advise me not, *O Moment*, to sit and worry;
They are my life, my childhood, those blue
hills.

For grown am I, can well see my plight,
A lot have I waned, though waxed in might,
Ensnare me not, *O Moment*, (when) you see me
hurry,
For the blue hills call and the sun shines
bright.

A Vernal Evening at the City Park

The leaves of trees waved to the wind,
I reclined on my grassy bed,
I tried to purge my tired mind
Of tedious phrases heard and said.
Dusk fell fast, the shadows grew,
Somewhere sang a sweet cuckoo.

My soul was seeking something green
At the end of concrete grey,
The living cushion beneath was keen
To rid me of my urban day.
Dusk fell fast, the shadows grew
To the song of the sweet cuckoo.

Like a stranger, a perfumed breeze
Brought me a sudden gust of glee,
Putting my troubled heart at ease,
As I felt something I didn't see.
Dusk fell fast, the shadows grew,
My heart she lulled, the sweet cuckoo.

The trees of green grew dark at last
With darkness now engulfing me,
And though my senses melted fast,
I smelt the green I couldn't see.
Dusk had fallen, the shadows too,
But still she sang, the sweet cuckoo.

To Shelley

Shelley! You are the deathless defender,
The champion of poets in flesh and blood,
Your poetry is no putrid pretender:
Through fluid verses, forceful flows its flood.

Shelley! The lightning in your lines is fierce,
And fiercer is the beauty of their chime,
Your thunder pulse did stop at thirty years,
Your sparkling spirit still sings on in rhyme.

Shelley! You are the voice of your West Wind,
The sylvan roar of Zephyrus you heard,
You shook and shattered with your untamed
mind
The fetters of the world through poetic word.

Shelley! Through Immortality's dream
The prophecy of freedom that you wove,
Unbound, unbowed, unconquered its gleam,
That won Prometheus liberty and love.

Shelley! When you sought the Skylark's song,
Into your voice her madness did she pour,
A portion of that nectar gift me now,
(That) in freedom to the heavens I can soar.

Shelley! The universal soul unites;
For even in the depth of despondence,
Your voice of volcanic hope ignites
In myriad minds fraternal concurrence.

The Stargazer

Laid back on the couch of a grassy patch,
He gazes at the vastness of the sky,
His wandering gaze browses the cosmos high,
Their twinkle in his starry eyes meets match.
What thoughts then do pervade his pensive
mind?
Is it the shallowness of ambition?
Restless, vain, and borne by blind occasion;
Is it, perhaps, a face, loving and kind?
The sky converses with the dazed beholder,
Mirroring the human world's bargains
Through billion bright beacons of the night,
The shining light conveys a hope yet bolder:
The emptying of all losses and of gains
Into the sea of wisdom, bliss and light.

The Chest of Life

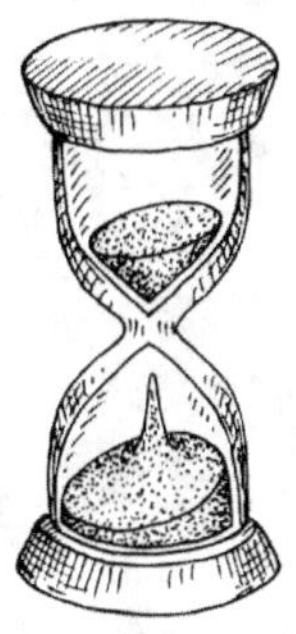

No matter what you hoard and hide,
The chest of life is void inside;
What you break, what you make,
What you store and what you take;

Your bargains will be cast aside.
The bargains will be cast aside.
All bargains will be cast aside.

The Song of Life

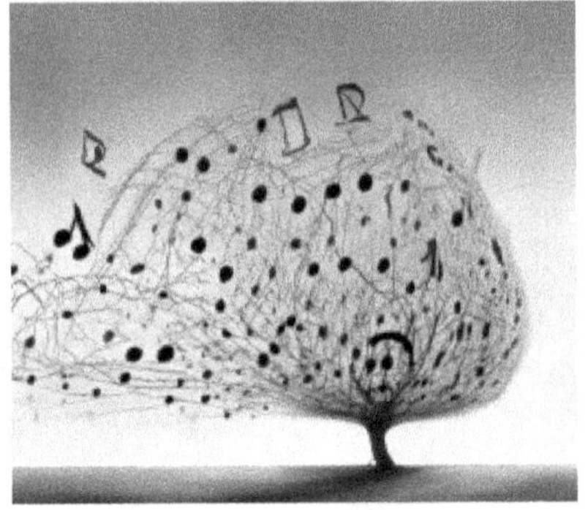

My heart shall beat for eternity;
It takes its cue and hums along,
For life is but an endless song
That brims with vivid variety.
Pure and true like Nature virgin
And serene as the morning dew,
Sparkling ever with melodies new,
The Song of Life is etched within.
Today's tunes are a bridge between
What is to come and what has been,
The joyous notes are ours to prize,
To know, to feel, to realise:
The beauty of a sunset lies
(In) the promise of a new sunrise.

The *Murali* and the Lotus

My heart was like a lonesome bird
Surrounded by the wilderness,
Until the *Murali* sweet arose
And carrying the Master's missive calm,
It poured forth its hypnotic notes,
And lo! I saw the Lotus gentle,
Across the distant seven skies;
The tempest within did subside.

Look! Night and day the *Murali* plays
And with His divine fingers sports,
The Divine Ten, fast as the mind,
And faster yet than *Marut*'s flight!
I hear, I hear the *Murali*'s call,
Distant as the divine Lotus,
(Its) mesmerising melody sweet,
Whose honeyed notes drench my soul.

While sages and savants covet
And aspire to comprehend Him,
I am that child who followed Love,
Knowing naught of wisdom's path.
Loving does the Lotus gaze,
Ecstatic roll the tears wild,
Vaasudev smiles; I reach His feet,
And turn my back on Heaven's call.